Learn Your Times Tables 2

Steve Mills and **Hilary Koll**

Name _____

Schofield & Sims

You will need a:

▶ pen or pencil

▶ stopwatch or clock with a second hand to time yourself.

For each times table:

▶ work through each page in order

▶ read the multiples aloud (use different voices or actions)

▶ look, cover, write, check several times

▶ learn the 'hard facts'

▶ cut out the cards from the centre of the book (pages C1 and C2) and practise with them

▶ ask someone to test you

▶ test yourself!

Contents

Ideas, games and activities

Tips for learning your tables

▶ Use different voices when you practise saying the tables facts. You could use the voice of a bird, a worm, a mouse or an elephant. Sometimes shout the facts, sometimes whisper them.

▶ Clap your hands, tap your head and jump around when you are saying your tables out loud.

Ideas for using the cut-out flashcards

▶ Keep the cards for each times table in an old envelope so that you don't lose them!

▶ Cut out the cards for one of the times tables. Spread out the cards on a surface, question-side up. Put them in order in a line, starting with **0**× going up to **10**×.

Say the multiples of that table aloud as you point to each card.

Then point to any card and give the answer, turning the card over to check. Repeat until you think you know them all.

▶ Use the cards for one of the times tables. Put them in a pile, question-side up. Answer the questions one at a time, turning the card over to check. Put the ones you get right into one pile and the ones you get wrong into another.

Then take each one you got wrong and say the question and answer out loud. Jump up and down as many times as the answer!

▶ Stick any cards you got wrong onto the fridge, bathroom mirror, in the car, or anywhere you will see it! Have a fact for the day and keep saying it over and over. Ask someone to keep asking you the fact and when you are sure that you know it you can put the card away!

▶ Ask someone in your family to hold the cards in one hand. Ask them to show you a question, holding it up so that they can see the answer on the back. See how quickly you can answer all the questions in a times table. Keep the ones you get wrong and practise them again until you know them.

The ×0, ×1, ×2, ×5, ×10 tables

×0 table

$0 \times 0 = 0$
$1 \times 0 = 0$
$2 \times 0 = 0$
$3 \times 0 = 0$
$4 \times 0 = 0$
$5 \times 0 = 0$
$6 \times 0 = 0$
$7 \times 0 = 0$
$8 \times 0 = 0$
$9 \times 0 = 0$
$10 \times 0 = 0$

×1 table

$0 \times 1 = 0$
$1 \times 1 = 1$
$2 \times 1 = 2$
$3 \times 1 = 3$
$4 \times 1 = 4$
$5 \times 1 = 5$
$6 \times 1 = 6$
$7 \times 1 = 7$
$8 \times 1 = 8$
$9 \times 1 = 9$
$10 \times 1 = 10$

×2 table

$0 \times 2 = 0$
$1 \times 2 = 2$
$2 \times 2 = 4$
$3 \times 2 = 6$
$4 \times 2 = 8$
$5 \times 2 = 10$
$6 \times 2 = 12$
$7 \times 2 = 14$
$8 \times 2 = 16$
$9 \times 2 = 18$
$10 \times 2 = 20$

×5 table

$0 \times 5 = 0$
$1 \times 5 = 5$
$2 \times 5 = 10$
$3 \times 5 = 15$
$4 \times 5 = 20$
$5 \times 5 = 25$
$6 \times 5 = 30$
$7 \times 5 = 35$
$8 \times 5 = 40$
$9 \times 5 = 45$
$10 \times 5 = 50$

×10 table

$0 \times 10 = 0$
$1 \times 10 = 10$
$2 \times 10 = 20$
$3 \times 10 = 30$
$4 \times 10 = 40$
$5 \times 10 = 50$
$6 \times 10 = 60$
$7 \times 10 = 70$
$8 \times 10 = 80$
$9 \times 10 = 90$
$10 \times 10 = 100$

What to notice

▶ A number **times zero** is **zero**.

▶ A number **times one** is **the number**.

▶ A number **times 2** is the same as **the number doubled**.

▶ Multiples of **10** end in **0**.

▶ Multiples of **5** end in **0** or **5**.

The mix-up man

For all multiplication questions, if you swap the numbers around the answer is the same. Look:

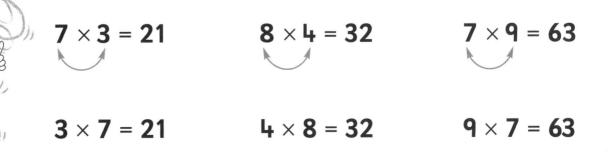

$7 \times 3 = 21$ $8 \times 4 = 32$ $7 \times 9 = 63$

$3 \times 7 = 21$ $4 \times 8 = 32$ $9 \times 7 = 63$

Get to know the ×3 table

The facts

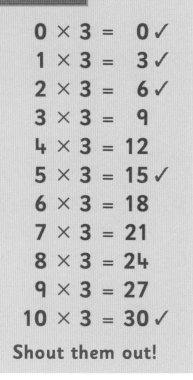

$0 \times 3 = 0$ ✓
$1 \times 3 = 3$ ✓
$2 \times 3 = 6$ ✓
$3 \times 3 = 9$
$4 \times 3 = 12$
$5 \times 3 = 15$ ✓
$6 \times 3 = 18$
$7 \times 3 = 21$
$8 \times 3 = 24$
$9 \times 3 = 27$
$10 \times 3 = 30$ ✓

Shout them out!

What to notice

▶ To learn the multiples of **3**, count using 'whisper, whisper, shout!'.
one, two, **three**!
four, five, **six**!
seven, eight, **nine**!
ten, eleven, **twelve**! and so on.

▶ Gradually make your whisper quieter until it can't be heard.

▶ An **even number times 3** will be **even**.

▶ An **odd number times 3** will be **odd**.

▶ You already know the ticked facts from your ×**0**, ×**1**, ×**2**, ×**10** and ×**5** tables.

Practise with the cards

Use the cut-out cards for the ×**3** table.

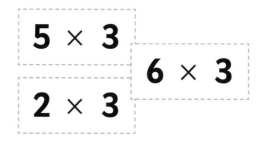

Put the cards in order.

Pick any card and say the answer. Turn over the card to check.

Now try these

Write the answers to these questions.

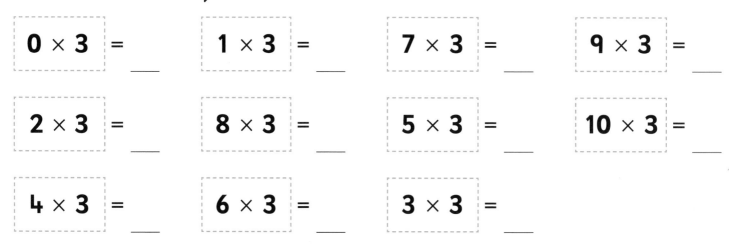

$0 \times 3 =$ _____

$1 \times 3 =$ _____

$7 \times 3 =$ _____

$9 \times 3 =$ _____

$2 \times 3 =$ _____

$8 \times 3 =$ _____

$5 \times 3 =$ _____

$10 \times 3 =$ _____

$4 \times 3 =$ _____

$6 \times 3 =$ _____

$3 \times 3 =$ _____

Hard facts

$3 \times 3 = 9$

Remember that **3 × 3** means **3 lots of 3**, which is **9**, not **3 + 3** which is **6**.

$6 \times 3 = 18$

6 lots of **3** is double **3** lots of **3**. Double **9** = **18**.

These three facts have answers in the **twenties**.

$7 \times 3 = 21$

Seven times three is **twenty-one**.

$8 \times 3 = 24$

Eight times three is **twenty-four**.

$9 \times 3 = 27$

Nine times three is **twenty-seven**.

Test yourself ×3 and 3×

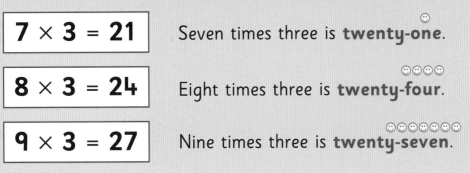

5 × 3 =	7 × 3 =	3 × 3 =	8 × 3 =
4 × 3 =	2 × 3 =	10 × 3 =	1 × 3 =
0 × 3 =	6 × 3 =	7 × 3 =	3 × 7 =
8 × 3 =	9 × 3 =	2 × 3 =	4 × 3 =
7 × 3 =	10 × 3 =	8 × 3 =	6 × 3 =
9 × 3 =	5 × 3 =	4 × 3 =	9 × 3 =
10 × 3 =	3 × 1 =	0 × 3 =	3 × 9 =
3 × 1 =	4 × 3 =	3 × 7 =	3 × 6 =
8 × 3 =	7 × 3 =	3 × 2 =	4 × 3 =
3 × 9 =	3 × 10 =	6 × 3 =	3 × 3 =
2 × 3 =	3 × 5 =	3 × 9 =	2 × 3 =

Time   Time   Time   Time

The facts

$0 \times 4 = 0$ ✓
$1 \times 4 = 4$ ✓
$2 \times 4 = 8$ ✓
$3 \times 4 = 12$ ✓
$4 \times 4 = 16$
$5 \times 4 = 20$ ✓
$6 \times 4 = 24$
$7 \times 4 = 28$
$8 \times 4 = 32$
$9 \times 4 = 36$
$10 \times 4 = 40$ ✓

Shout them out!

What to notice

▶ All the answers in the ×4 table are **even** numbers.

▶ **No** answer in the ×4 table will end in **1**, **3**, **5**, **7**, or **9**.

▶ The answers are **double** the answers in the ×2 table.

$7 \times 2 = 14$

$7 \times 4 = $ **double** $14 = 28$

▶ You already know the ticked facts from the ×**0**, ×**1**, ×**2**, ×**5**, ×**10** and ×**3** tables.

Practise with the cards

Use the cut-out cards for the ×4 table.

Put the cards in order.

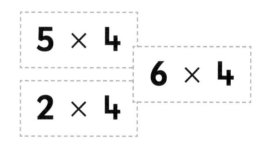

Pick any card and say the answer. Turn over the card to check.

Now try these

Write the answers to these questions.

$2 \times 4 = $ ____

$5 \times 4 = $ ____

$6 \times 4 = $ ____

$3 \times 4 = $ ____

$1 \times 4 = $ ____

$10 \times 4 = $ ____

$4 \times 4 = $ ____

$9 \times 4 = $ ____

$0 \times 4 = $ ____

$7 \times 4 = $ ____

$8 \times 4 = $ ____

The ×4 table

Hard facts

$3 \times 4 = 12$

Notice that this fact has digits **1**, **2**, **3** and **4**.
Say aloud the rhyme
3, 4 ... 12 is the same as 3 times 4.

$4 \times 4 = 16$

Think of a square with **4** rows of **4** beans.
Whisper the rhyme
4 times 4 beans are 16.

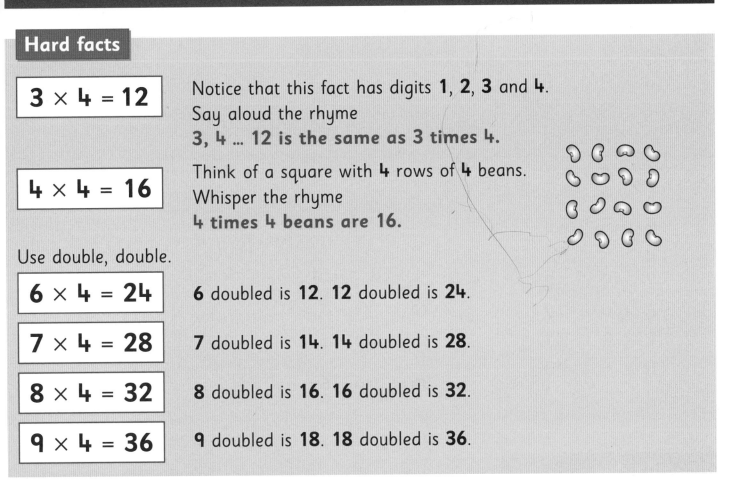

Use double, double.

$6 \times 4 = 24$ **6** doubled is **12**. **12** doubled is **24**.

$7 \times 4 = 28$ **7** doubled is **14**. **14** doubled is **28**.

$8 \times 4 = 32$ **8** doubled is **16**. **16** doubled is **32**.

$9 \times 4 = 36$ **9** doubled is **18**. **18** doubled is **36**.

Test yourself

×4 and 4×

$5 \times 4 =$	$7 \times 4 =$	$3 \times 4 =$	$8 \times 4 =$
$3 \times 4 =$	$2 \times 4 =$	$10 \times 4 =$	$1 \times 4 =$
$0 \times 4 =$	$6 \times 4 =$	$7 \times 4 =$	$4 \times 7 =$
$8 \times 4 =$	$9 \times 4 =$	$2 \times 4 =$	$3 \times 4 =$
$7 \times 4 =$	$10 \times 4 =$	$8 \times 4 =$	$6 \times 4 =$
$9 \times 4 =$	$5 \times 4 =$	$4 \times 4 =$	$9 \times 4 =$
$10 \times 4 =$	$4 \times 1 =$	$0 \times 4 =$	$4 \times 9 =$
$4 \times 1 =$	$4 \times 4 =$	$4 \times 7 =$	$4 \times 6 =$
$8 \times 4 =$	$7 \times 4 =$	$4 \times 2 =$	$4 \times 4 =$
$4 \times 9 =$	$4 \times 10 =$	$6 \times 4 =$	$3 \times 4 =$
$4 \times 4 =$	$2 \times 4 =$	$4 \times 4 =$	$4 \times 8 =$
Time	Time	Time	Time

Get to know the ×9 table

The facts

$$0 \times 9 = 0 \checkmark$$
$$1 \times 9 = 9 \checkmark$$
$$2 \times 9 = 18 \checkmark$$
$$3 \times 9 = 27 \checkmark$$
$$4 \times 9 = 36 \checkmark$$
$$5 \times 9 = 45 \checkmark$$
$$6 \times 9 = 54$$
$$7 \times 9 = 63$$
$$8 \times 9 = 72$$
$$9 \times 9 = 81$$
$$10 \times 9 = 90 \checkmark$$

Shout them out!

What to notice

▶ It is best to learn the ×9 table before the ×6, ×7 and ×8 tables because it's **easier**!

▶ The picture below shows you what to do with your fingers to help you find the answers to any ×9 or 9× question really quickly.

▶ Notice that the digits of these multiples of 9 add up to 9.

18	$1 + 8 = 9$
27	$2 + 7 = 9$
36	$3 + 6 = 9$ and so on.

Learning the ×9 table

▶ Hold your palms towards you.

▶ For 3×9 or 9×3 hold down your **third** finger from the left.

The fingers to the **left** of the bent finger are each worth **10**.

The fingers to the **right** of the bent finger are each worth 1.

▶ For 4×9 or 9×4 hold down your **fourth** finger and so on.

▶ It works for all the 9 times table!

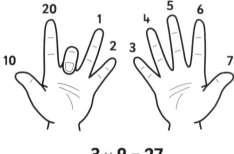

$$3 \times 9 = 27$$

$$4 \times 9 = 36$$

$$7 \times 9 = 63$$

$$8 \times 9 = 72$$

Try it yourself!

The ×9 table

Look, cover, write, check

Look at the correct answers. **Cover** them. **Write** the answers. Now **check**. Repeat three times.

0 × 9 = 0	0 × 9 =	0 × 9 =	0 × 9 =
1 × 9 = 9	1 × 9 =	1 × 9 =	1 × 9 =
2 × 9 = 18	2 × 9 =	2 × 9 =	2 × 9 =
3 × 9 = 27	3 × 9 =	3 × 9 =	3 × 9 =
4 × 9 = 36	4 × 9 =	4 × 9 =	4 × 9 =
5 × 9 = 45	5 × 9 =	5 × 9 =	5 × 9 =
6 × 9 = 54	6 × 9 =	6 × 9 =	6 × 9 =
7 × 9 = 63	7 × 9 =	7 × 9 =	7 × 9 =
8 × 9 = 72	8 × 9 =	8 × 9 =	8 × 9 =
9 × 9 = 81	9 × 9 =	9 × 9 =	9 × 9 =
10 × 9 = 90	10 × 9 =	10 × 9 =	10 × 9 =

Practise with the cards

Use the cut-out cards for the ×9 table.

Put the cards in order.

4 × 9

9 × 9

7 × 9

Pick any card and say the answer. Turn over the card to check.

Now try these

Write the answers to these questions.

5 × 9 =

6 × 9 =

2 × 9 =

7 × 9 =

1 × 9 =

4 × 9 =

0 × 9 =

8 × 9 =

10 × 9 =

3 × 9 =

Hard facts

There are **no** hard facts for the ×9 table if you learn to use your fingers!
Practise these.

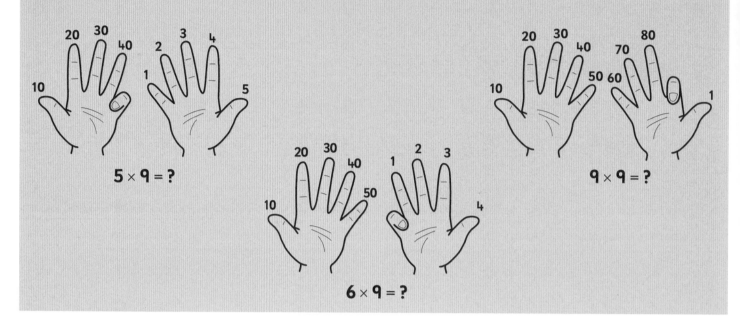

$5 \times 9 = ?$

$6 \times 9 = ?$

$9 \times 9 = ?$

Chloe's test

Chloe has got some of these answers wrong!

Tick which of Chloe's answers are correct.

Cross those that are wrong and write the correct answer.

$3 \times 9 = 27$ ✓

$7 \times 9 = 45$ ✗ 63

Name: Chloe		$3 \times 9 = 27$	$7 \times 9 = 45$
$9 \times 9 = 81$	$6 \times 9 = 54$	$4 \times 9 = 35$	$10 \times 9 = 90$
$2 \times 9 = 29$	$0 \times 9 = 9$	$1 \times 9 = 9$	$5 \times 9 = 40$
$6 \times 9 = 45$	$8 \times 9 = 81$	$4 \times 9 = 36$	$7 \times 9 = 63$
$3 \times 9 = 30$	$0 \times 9 = 0$	$9 \times 9 = 90$	$5 \times 9 = 45$
$2 \times 9 = 18$	$8 \times 9 = 72$		Score: _____ out of 20

×9 and 9×

7 × 9 =	10 × 9 =	8 × 9 =	6 × 9 =
3 × 9 =	2 × 9 =	10 × 9 =	1 × 9 =
4 × 9 =	7 × 9 =	3 × 9 =	8 × 9 =
0 × 9 =	6 × 9 =	7 × 9 =	7 × 9 =
8 × 9 =	9 × 9 =	2 × 9 =	3 × 9 =
2 × 9 =	0 × 9 =	1 × 9 =	0 × 9 =
9 × 9 =	5 × 9 =	4 × 9 =	9 × 9 =
6 × 9 =	3 × 9 =	6 × 9 =	10 × 9 =
10 × 9 =	4 × 9 =	9 × 9 =	5 × 9 =
5 × 9 =	1 × 9 =	5 × 9 =	4 × 9 =
1 × 9 =	8 × 9 =	0 × 9 =	2 × 9 =

Time	Time	Time	Time

Here the mix-up man has turned some of the tables.

9 × 10 =	9 × 3 =	0 × 9 =	9 × 9 =
9 × 1 =	4 × 9 =	9 × 9 =	9 × 6 =
8 × 9 =	7 × 9 =	9 × 2 =	9 × 4 =
9 × 9 =	10 × 9 =	6 × 9 =	3 × 9 =
9 × 4 =	9 × 2 =	4 × 9 =	9 × 8 =
2 × 9 =	5 × 9 =	9 × 7 =	2 × 9 =
9 × 6 =	9 × 9 =	9 × 10 =	9 × 0 =
7 × 9 =	9 × 0 =	9 × 1 =	10 × 9 =
5 × 9 =	8 × 9 =	3 × 9 =	9 × 1 =
3 × 9 =	9 × 6 =	5 × 9 =	9 × 5 =
9 × 0 =	1 × 9 =	8 × 9 =	9 × 7 =

Time	Time	Time	Time

The facts

$$0 \times 6 = 0 ✓$$
$$1 \times 6 = 6 ✓$$
$$2 \times 6 = 12 ✓$$
$$3 \times 6 = 18 ✓$$
$$4 \times 6 = 24 ✓$$
$$5 \times 6 = 30 ✓$$
$$6 \times 6 = 36$$
$$7 \times 6 = 42$$
$$8 \times 6 = 48$$
$$9 \times 6 = 54 ✓$$
$$10 \times 6 = 60 ✓$$

Shout them out!

What to notice

▶ All the multiples of **6** are **even**.

▶ If you know your ×**0**, ×**1**, ×**2**, ×**3**, ×**4**, ×**5**, ×**9** and ×**10** tables then there are only **three facts** in the ×**6** table left to learn! All the facts that are ticked are ones that you know from other tables. For example, you know that **6 × 9 = 54** so **9 × 6** is the same!

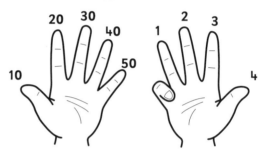

Getting to know the multiples of 6

Write these **multiples** of **6** in order, starting with **6**.

| 48 | 24 | 6 | 18 | 30 | 36 | 54 | 60 | 12 | 42 |

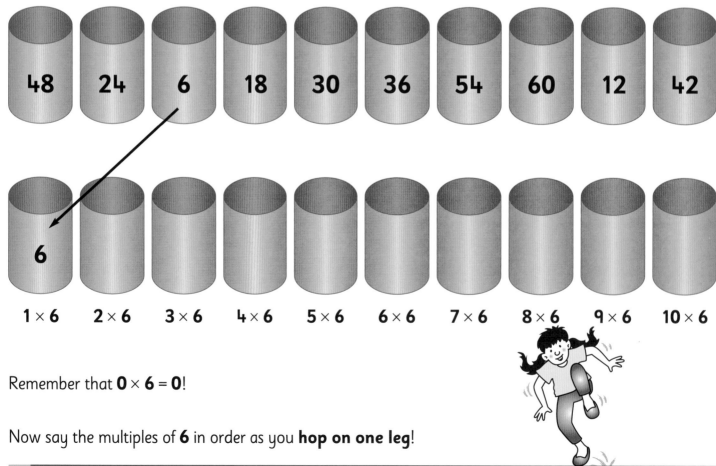

6									
1 × 6	2 × 6	3 × 6	4 × 6	5 × 6	6 × 6	7 × 6	8 × 6	9 × 6	10 × 6

Remember that **0 × 6 = 0**!

Now say the multiples of **6** in order as you **hop on one leg**!

Pull-out answers

Page 6

$0 \times 3 = 0$ $1 \times 3 = 3$ $7 \times 3 = 21$ $9 \times 3 = 27$

$2 \times 3 = 6$ $8 \times 3 = 24$ $5 \times 3 = 15$ $10 \times 3 = 30$

$4 \times 3 = 12$ $6 \times 3 = 18$ $3 \times 3 = 9$

Page 7

15	21	9	24
12	6	30	3
0	18	21	21
24	27	6	12
21	30	24	18
27	15	12	27
30	3	0	27
3	12	21	18
24	21	6	12
27	30	18	9
6	15	27	6

Page 8

$2 \times 4 = 8$ $5 \times 4 = 20$ $6 \times 4 = 24$ $3 \times 4 = 12$

$1 \times 4 = 4$ $10 \times 4 = 40$ $4 \times 4 = 16$ $9 \times 4 = 36$

$0 \times 4 = 0$ $7 \times 4 = 28$ $8 \times 4 = 32$

Page 9

20	28	12	32
12	8	40	4
0	24	28	28
32	36	8	12
28	40	32	24
36	20	16	36
40	4	0	36
4	16	28	24
32	28	8	16
36	40	24	12
16	8	16	32

Page 11

$5 \times 9 = 45$ $6 \times 9 = 54$

$2 \times 9 = 18$ $7 \times 9 = 63$ $1 \times 9 = 9$ $4 \times 9 = 36$

$0 \times 9 = 0$ $8 \times 9 = 72$ $10 \times 9 = 90$ $3 \times 9 = 27$

Page 12 – Hard facts

$5 \times 9 = 45$ $6 \times 9 = 54$ $9 \times 9 = 81$

Chloe's test

$7 \times 9 = 63$ $4 \times 9 = 36$ $2 \times 9 = 18$ $0 \times 9 = 0$

$5 \times 9 = 45$ $6 \times 9 = 54$ $8 \times 9 = 72$ $3 \times 9 = 27$

$9 \times 9 = 81$

Chloe scores **11/20**

Page 13

63	90	72	54
27	18	90	9
36	63	27	72
0	54	63	63
72	81	18	27
18	0	9	0
81	45	36	81
54	27	54	90

90	36	81	45
45	9	45	36
9	72	0	18

90	27	0	81
9	36	81	54
72	63	18	36
81	90	54	27
36	18	36	72
18	45	63	18
54	81	90	0
63	0	9	90
45	72	27	9
27	54	45	45
0	9	72	63

Page 15

$10 \times 6 = 60$ $3 \times 6 = 18$

$6 \times 6 = 36$ $2 \times 6 = 12$ $7 \times 6 = 42$ $8 \times 6 = 48$

$0 \times 6 = 0$ $5 \times 6 = 30$ $4 \times 6 = 24$ $9 \times 6 = 54$

Page 16

$4 \times 6 = 24$ $7 \times 6 = 42$ $6 \times 6 = 36$ $3 \times 6 = 18$

$9 \times 6 = 54$ $8 \times 6 = 48$

Page 17

24	42	18	48
18	12	60	6
0	36	42	42
48	54	12	18
42	60	48	36
54	30	24	54
36	18	30	60
12	0	6	0
60	24	54	30
30	6	36	24
6	48	0	12

60	6	0	54
6	24	42	30
48	42	12	24
54	60	36	18
24	12	24	48
12	36	54	12
30	54	60	0
42	0	6	60
36	48	18	6
18	30	30	36
0	18	48	42

Page 18

35	7	49	
28	63		
56	42	70	21

Page 19

$2 \times 7 = 14$ $5 \times 7 = 35$

$6 \times 7 = 42$ $3 \times 7 = 21$ $7 \times 7 = 49$ $8 \times 7 = 56$

$0 \times 7 = 0$ $10 \times 7 = 70$ $4 \times 7 = 28$ $9 \times 7 = 63$

Pull-out answers

Page **20**

9×7 = sixty-three $\qquad$ 7×7 = forty-nine

4×7 = twenty-eight $\qquad$ 8×7 = fifty-six

6×7 = forty-two $\qquad$ 3×7 = twenty-one

Page **21**

35	28	21	56
21	14	70	7
0	42	49	49
56	63	14	21
28	70	56	42
63	35	28	63
42	21	42	70
14	0	7	0
70	49	63	35
49	7	35	28
7	56	0	14

70	7	0	63
7	49	49	42
56	28	14	28
63	70	42	21
28	14	28	56
14	35	63	14
42	63	70	0
49	0	7	70
35	56	21	7
21	42	35	35
0	21	56	49

Page **23**

0×8 = 0 $\qquad$ 9×8 = 72

7×8 = 56 $\qquad$ 3×8 = 24 $\qquad$ 6×8 = 48 $\qquad$ 4×8 = 32

1×8 = 8 $\qquad$ 10×8 = 80 $\qquad$ 8×8 = 64 $\qquad$ 5×8 = 40

Page **24**

8×8 = 64 $\qquad$ 3×8 = 24 $\qquad$ 7×8 = 56

9×8 = 72 $\qquad$ 6×8 = 48 $\qquad$ 4×8 = 32

Page **25**

40	32	24	56
24	16	80	8
0	48	56	64
64	72	16	24
32	80	64	48
72	40	32	72
48	24	48	80
16	0	8	0
80	56	72	40
56	8	40	32
8	64	0	16

80	8	0	72
8	64	56	48
56	32	16	32
72	80	48	24
32	16	32	56
16	40	72	16

48	72	80	0
64	0	8	80
40	56	24	8
24	48	40	40
0	24	64	64

Page **26**

12	8	16	60
70	30	9	14
30	27	36	8
35	30	40	54
80	24	21	25
32	0	20	42
49	16	18	100
12	72	42	8
0	48	28	56
36	32	24	18
63	81	64	35

18	28	20	10
12	48	50	40
0	35	15	63
45	27	63	40
54	45	24	21
24	25	36	16
32	9	54	56
56	48	42	36
49	64	72	48
63	42	28	27
48	32	81	64

Page **27**

35	30	40	54
0	48	28	56
12	72	42	8
70	30	9	14
32	0	20	42
30	27	36	8
80	24	21	25
49	16	18	100
63	81	64	35
12	8	16	60
36	32	24	18

24	25	36	16
18	28	20	10
12	48	50	40
49	64	72	48
45	27	63	40
32	9	54	56
0	35	15	63
54	45	24	21
56	48	42	36
48	32	81	64
63	42	28	27

×8 table	×7 table	×6 table	×9 table	×4 table	×3 table
0 × 8	0 × 7	0 × 6	0 × 9	0 × 4	0 × 3
1 × 8	1 × 7	1 × 6	1 × 9	1 × 4	1 × 3
2 × 8	2 × 7	2 × 6	2 × 9	2 × 4	2 × 3
3 × 8	3 × 7	3 × 6	3 × 9	3 × 4	3 × 3
4 × 8	4 × 7	4 × 6	4 × 9	4 × 4	4 × 3
5 × 8	5 × 7	5 × 6	5 × 9	5 × 4	5 × 3
6 × 8	6 × 7	6 × 6	6 × 9	6 × 4	6 × 3
7 × 8	7 × 7	7 × 6	7 × 9	7 × 4	7 × 3
8 × 8	8 × 7	8 × 6	8 × 9	8 × 4	8 × 3
9 × 8	9 × 7	9 × 6	9 × 9	9 × 4	9 × 3
10 × 8	10 × 7	10 × 6	10 × 9	10 × 4	10 × 3

×3 table	×4 table	×9 table	×6 table	×7 table	×8 table
0	0	0	0	0	0
3	4	9	6	7	8
6	8	18	12	14	16
9	12	27	18	21	24
12	16	36	24	28	32
15	20	45	30	35	40
18	24	54	36	42	48
21	28	63	42	49	56
24	32	72	48	56	64
27	36	81	54	63	72
30	40	90	60	70	80

Schofield & Sims Learn Your Times Tables 2

The ×6 table

Look, cover, write, check

Look at the correct answers. **Cover** them. **Write** the answers. Now **check**. Repeat three times.

$0 \times 6 = 0$	$0 \times 6 =$	$0 \times 6 =$	$0 \times 6 =$
$1 \times 6 = 6$	$1 \times 6 =$	$1 \times 6 =$	$1 \times 6 =$
$2 \times 6 = 12$	$2 \times 6 =$	$2 \times 6 =$	$2 \times 6 =$
$3 \times 6 = 18$	$3 \times 6 =$	$3 \times 6 =$	$3 \times 6 =$
$4 \times 6 = 24$	$4 \times 6 =$	$4 \times 6 =$	$4 \times 6 =$
$5 \times 6 = 30$	$5 \times 6 =$	$5 \times 6 =$	$5 \times 6 =$
$6 \times 6 = 36$	$6 \times 6 =$	$6 \times 6 =$	$6 \times 6 =$
$7 \times 6 = 42$	$7 \times 6 =$	$7 \times 6 =$	$7 \times 6 =$
$8 \times 6 = 48$	$8 \times 6 =$	$8 \times 6 =$	$8 \times 6 =$
$9 \times 6 = 54$	$9 \times 6 =$	$9 \times 6 =$	$9 \times 6 =$
$10 \times 6 = 60$	$10 \times 6 =$	$10 \times 6 =$	$10 \times 6 =$

Practise with the cards

Use the cut-out cards for the ×**6** table.

Put the cards in order.

8×6

3×6

7×6

Pick any card and say the answer. Turn over the card to check.

Now try these

Write the answers to these questions.

$10 \times 6 =$ ____ $3 \times 6 =$ ____

$6 \times 6 =$ ____ $2 \times 6 =$ ____ $7 \times 6 =$ ____ $8 \times 6 =$ ____

$0 \times 6 =$ ____ $5 \times 6 =$ ____ $4 \times 6 =$ ____ $9 \times 6 =$ ____

The ×6 table

Hard facts

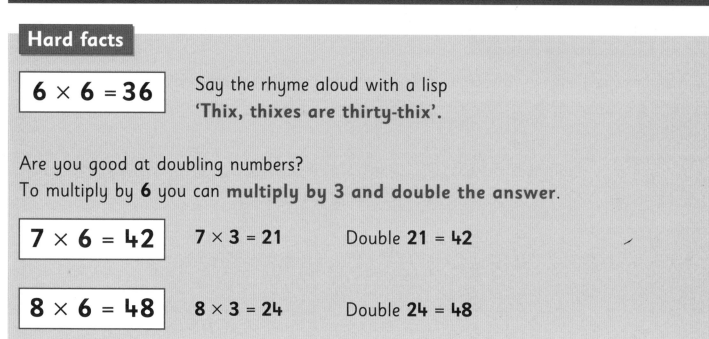

$6 \times 6 = 36$

Say the rhyme aloud with a lisp
'Thix, thixes are thirty-thix'.

Are you good at doubling numbers?
To multiply by **6** you can **multiply by 3 and double the answer**.

$7 \times 6 = 42$ $7 \times 3 = 21$ Double **21** = **42**

$8 \times 6 = 48$ $8 \times 3 = 24$ Double **24** = **48**

Which dog?

Draw lines to join each dog to its owner. See how quickly you can do this.

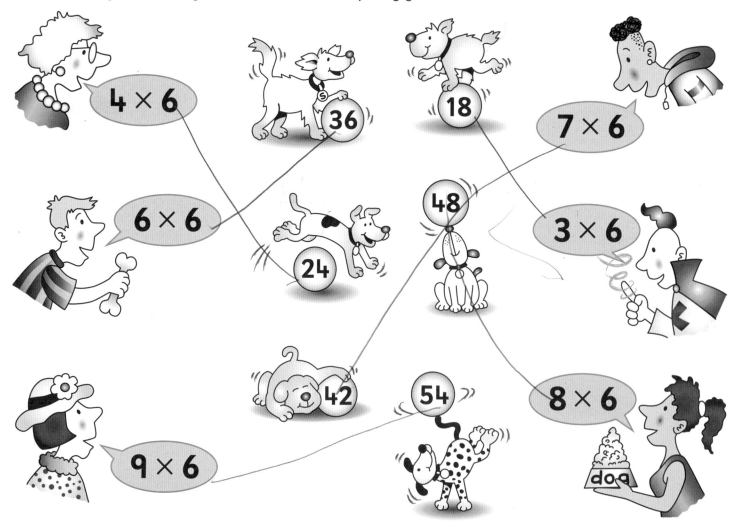

4 × 6 = 21	7 × 6 = 42	3 × 6 =	8 × 6 =
3 × 6 = 18	2 × 6 = 12	10 × 6 =	1 × 6 =
0 × 6 = 0	6 × 6 = 36	7 × 6 =	7 × 6 =
8 × 6 = 50 ⁰48	9 × 6 = 54	2 × 6 =	3 × 6 =
7 × 6 = 42	10 × 6 = 60	8 × 6 =	6 × 6 =
9 × 6 = 54	5 × 6 = 30	4 × 6 =	9 × 6 =
6 × 6 = 36	3 × 6 = 18	5 × 6 =	10 × 6 =
2 × 6 = 12	0 × 6 = 0	1 × 6 =	0 × 6 =
10 × 6 = 60	4 × 6 = 28 24	9 × 6 =	5 × 6 =
5 × 6 = 30	1 × 6 = 6	6 × 6 =	4 × 6 =
1 × 6 = 6	8 × 6 = 48	0 × 6 =	2 × 6 =

Time 1 min: 50   Time 1 min: 20   Time ____   Time ____

Here the mix-up man has turned some of the tables.

10 × 6 =	6 × 1 =	0 × 6 =	6 × 9 =
6 × 1 =	4 × 6 =	6 × 7 =	5 × 6 =
8 × 6 =	7 × 6 =	6 × 2 =	6 × 4 =
6 × 9 =	6 × 10 =	6 × 6 =	3 × 6 =
6 × 4 =	2 × 6 =	4 × 6 =	6 × 8 =
2 × 6 =	6 × 6 =	6 × 9 =	2 × 6 =
6 × 5 =	9 × 6 =	10 × 6 =	6 × 0 =
7 × 6 =	6 × 0 =	6 × 1 =	10 × 6 =
6 × 6 =	8 × 6 =	3 × 6 =	6 × 1 =
3 × 6 =	6 × 5 =	5 × 6 =	6 × 6 =
6 × 0 =	3 × 6 =	8 × 6 =	6 × 7 =

Time ____   Time ____   Time ____   Time ____

Get to know the ×7 table

The facts

0 × 7 =   0 ✓
1 × 7 =   7 ✓
2 × 7 = 14 ✓
3 × 7 = 21 ✓
4 × 7 = 28 ✓
5 × 7 = 35 ✓
6 × 7 = 42 ✓
7 × 7 = 49
8 × 7 = 56
9 × 7 = 63 ✓
10 × 7 = 70 ✓

Shout them out!

What to notice

▶ If you know your ×0, ×1, ×2, ×3, ×4, ×5, ×6, ×9 and ×10 tables, then there are only two facts in the ×7 table left to learn! All the facts that are ticked are ones that you know from other tables.

Getting to know the multiples of 7

The first ten **multiples** of **7** are shown in blue under this line. Say the **multiples of 7** aloud.

×7	0	1	2	3	4	5	6	7	8	9	10
	0	7	14	21	28	35	42	49	56	63	70

Circle the numbers below that are **multiples** of **7**.

27	35	32	12	48	7	49
28	63	19	40	26	54	
36	56	29	42	70	21	64

Now say the multiples of **7** in order while **patting yourself on your head and rubbing your tummy at the same time!**

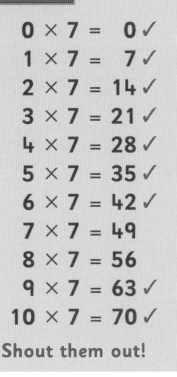

The ×7 table

Look, cover, write, check

Look at the correct answers. **Cover** them. **Write** the answers. Now **check**. Repeat three times.

0 × 7 = 0	0 × 7 =	0 × 7 =	0 × 7 =
1 × 7 = 7	1 × 7 =	1 × 7 =	1 × 7 =
2 × 7 = 14	2 × 7 =	2 × 7 =	2 × 7 =
3 × 7 = 21	3 × 7 =	3 × 7 =	3 × 7 =
4 × 7 = 28	4 × 7 =	4 × 7 =	4 × 7 =
5 × 7 = 35	5 × 7 =	5 × 7 =	5 × 7 =
6 × 7 = 42	6 × 7 =	6 × 7 =	6 × 7 =
7 × 7 = 49	7 × 7 =	7 × 7 =	7 × 7 =
8 × 7 = 56	8 × 7 =	8 × 7 =	8 × 7 =
9 × 7 = 63	9 × 7 =	9 × 7 =	9 × 7 =
10 × 7 = 70	10 × 7 =	10 × 7 =	10 × 7 =

Practise with the cards

Use the cut-out cards for the ×**7** table.

9 × 7

7 × 7

Put the cards in order.

8 × 7

Pick any card and say the answer. Turn over the card to check.

Now try these

Write the answers to these questions.

2 × 7 =

5 × 7 =

6 × 7 =

3 × 7 =

7 × 7 =

8 × 7 =

0 × 7 =

10 × 7 =

4 × 7 =

9 × 7 =

The ×7 table

Hard facts

$8 \times 7 = 56$

This fact has the same answer as

$7 \times 8 = 56$

Notice that this fact has digits **5**, **6**, **7** and **8**.

Say aloud the rhyme

5, 6, 7, 8, seven eights are fifty-six.

$7 \times 7 = 49$

Think of a square field with
7 rows of **7** pine trees.

Whisper the rhyme

7 lots of 7 pines are 49.

Which question?

Draw lines to show who is answering each question.

9 × 7

7 × 7

4 × 7

8 × 7

6 × 7

3 × 7

forty-two

twenty-eight

forty-nine

twenty-one

fifty-six

sixty-three

$5 \times 7 =$ ▢ $4 \times 7 =$ ▢ $3 \times 7 =$ ▢ $8 \times 7 =$ ▢

$3 \times 7 =$ ▢ $2 \times 7 =$ ▢ $10 \times 7 =$ ▢ $1 \times 7 =$ ▢

$0 \times 7 =$ ▢ $6 \times 7 =$ ▢ $7 \times 7 =$ ▢ $7 \times 7 =$ ▢

$8 \times 7 =$ ▢ $9 \times 7 =$ ▢ $2 \times 7 =$ ▢ $3 \times 7 =$ ▢

$4 \times 7 =$ ▢ $10 \times 7 =$ ▢ $8 \times 7 =$ ▢ $6 \times 7 =$ ▢

$9 \times 7 =$ ▢ $5 \times 7 =$ ▢ $4 \times 7 =$ ▢ $9 \times 7 =$ ▢

$6 \times 7 =$ ▢ $3 \times 7 =$ ▢ $6 \times 7 =$ ▢ $10 \times 7 =$ ▢

$2 \times 7 =$ ▢ $0 \times 7 =$ ▢ $1 \times 7 =$ ▢ $0 \times 7 =$ ▢

$10 \times 7 =$ ▢ $7 \times 7 =$ ▢ $9 \times 7 =$ ▢ $5 \times 7 =$ ▢

$7 \times 7 =$ ▢ $1 \times 7 =$ ▢ $5 \times 7 =$ ▢ $4 \times 7 =$ ▢

$1 \times 7 =$ ▢ $8 \times 7 =$ ▢ $0 \times 7 =$ ▢ $2 \times 7 =$ ▢

Time ▢   Time ▢   Time ▢   Time ▢

Here the mix-up man has turned some of the tables.

$10 \times 7 =$ ▢ $7 \times 1 =$ ▢ $0 \times 7 =$ ▢ $7 \times 9 =$ ▢

$7 \times 1 =$ ▢ $7 \times 7 =$ ▢ $7 \times 7 =$ ▢ $7 \times 6 =$ ▢

$8 \times 7 =$ ▢ $7 \times 4 =$ ▢ $7 \times 2 =$ ▢ $4 \times 7 =$ ▢

$7 \times 9 =$ ▢ $7 \times 10 =$ ▢ $6 \times 7 =$ ▢ $3 \times 7 =$ ▢

$4 \times 7 =$ ▢ $2 \times 7 =$ ▢ $4 \times 7 =$ ▢ $7 \times 8 =$ ▢

$2 \times 7 =$ ▢ $7 \times 5 =$ ▢ $7 \times 9 =$ ▢ $2 \times 7 =$ ▢

$7 \times 6 =$ ▢ $9 \times 7 =$ ▢ $10 \times 7 =$ ▢ $7 \times 0 =$ ▢

$7 \times 7 =$ ▢ $7 \times 0 =$ ▢ $7 \times 1 =$ ▢ $10 \times 7 =$ ▢

$7 \times 5 =$ ▢ $8 \times 7 =$ ▢ $3 \times 7 =$ ▢ $7 \times 1 =$ ▢

$3 \times 7 =$ ▢ $7 \times 6 =$ ▢ $7 \times 5 =$ ▢ $5 \times 7 =$ ▢

$7 \times 0 =$ ▢ $3 \times 7 =$ ▢ $8 \times 7 =$ ▢ $7 \times 7 =$ ▢

Time ▢   Time ▢   Time ▢   Time ▢

Get to know the ×8 table

The facts

$$0 \times 8 = 0 \checkmark$$
$$1 \times 8 = 8 \checkmark$$
$$2 \times 8 = 16 \checkmark$$
$$3 \times 8 = 24 \checkmark$$
$$4 \times 8 = 32 \checkmark$$
$$5 \times 8 = 40 \checkmark$$
$$6 \times 8 = 48 \checkmark$$
$$7 \times 8 = 56 \checkmark$$
$$8 \times 8 = 64$$
$$9 \times 8 = 72 \checkmark$$
$$10 \times 8 = 80 \checkmark$$

Shout them out!

What to notice

▶ All the answers in the ×8 table are even numbers.
▶ The answers can be found using double, double, double, like this:

$6 \times 8 = ?$
double 6 = 12
double 12 = 24
double 24 = 48   **$6 \times 8 = 48$**

▶ If you know your ×0, ×1, ×2, ×3, ×4, ×5, ×6, ×7, ×9 and ×10 tables then there is only **one fact** in the ×8 table left to learn! All the facts that are ticked are ones that you know from other tables.

Getting to know the multiples of 8

The first ten **multiples of 8** are shown in the snake. Say them in order out loud.
Cover a number with a coin and say them all again in order.
Keep going until all the numbers are covered with coins!
Can you remember all the hidden numbers?

8   16   24   32   40   48   56   64   72   80

Schofield & Sims Learn Your Times Tables 2

The ×8 table

Look, cover, write, check

Look at the correct answers. **Cover** them. **Write** the answers. Now **check**. Repeat three times.

0 × 8 = 0	0 × 8 =	0 × 8 =	0 × 8 =
1 × 8 = 8	1 × 8 =	1 × 8 =	1 × 8 =
2 × 8 = 16	2 × 8 =	2 × 8 =	2 × 8 =
3 × 8 = 24	3 × 8 =	3 × 8 =	3 × 8 =
4 × 8 = 32	4 × 8 =	4 × 8 =	4 × 8 =
5 × 8 = 40	5 × 8 =	5 × 8 =	5 × 8 =
6 × 8 = 48	6 × 8 =	6 × 8 =	6 × 8 =
7 × 8 = 56	7 × 8 =	7 × 8 =	7 × 8 =
8 × 8 = 64	8 × 8 =	8 × 8 =	8 × 8 =
9 × 8 = 72	9 × 8 =	9 × 8 =	9 × 8 =
10 × 8 = 80	10 × 8 =	10 × 8 =	10 × 8 =

Practise with the cards

Use the cut-out cards for the ×8 table.

9 × 8

7 × 8

Put the cards in order.

8 × 8

Pick any card and say the answer. Turn over the card to check.

Now try these

Write the answers to these questions.

0 × 8 =

9 × 8 =

7 × 8 =

3 × 8 =

6 × 8 =

4 × 8 =

1 × 8 =

10 × 8 =

8 × 8 =

5 × 8 =

The ×8 table

Hard facts

$6 \times 8 = 48$ This fact has the same answer as $8 \times 6 = 48$

Remember you can multiply by **6** by **multiplying by 3** and then **doubling**.

$8 \times 3 = 24$ Double **24 = 48**

$7 \times 8 = 56$ Notice that this fact has digits **5, 6, 7** and **8**.

Say aloud the rhyme

5, 6, 7, 8, seven eights are fifty-six.

$8 \times 8 = 64$ Think of a monster with **8** arms.

On each arm of the monster there are **8** claws.

Shout the rhyme

8 arms with 8 claws is 64!

Which kite?

Draw lines to join each kite to its owner. See how quickly you can do this.

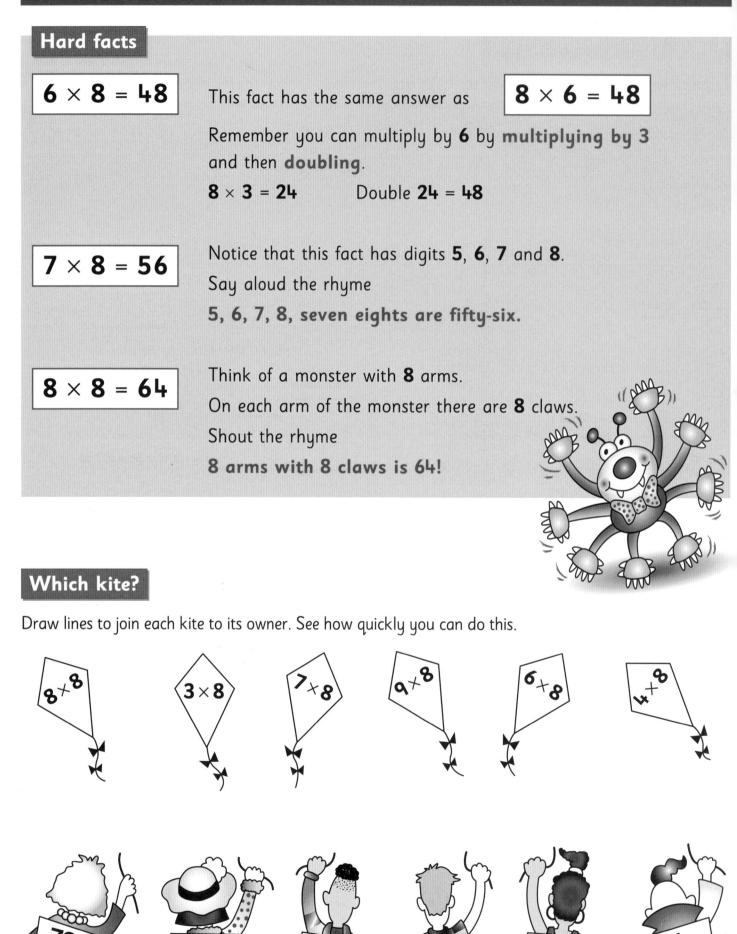

8 × 8   3 × 8   7 × 8   9 × 8   6 × 8   4 × 8

72   56   64   48   32   24

Schofield & Sims **Learn Your Times Tables 2**

5 × 8 = ☐   4 × 8 = ☐   3 × 8 = ☐   7 × 8 = ☐

3 × 8 = ☐   2 × 8 = ☐   10 × 8 = ☐   1 × 8 = ☐

0 × 8 = ☐   6 × 8 = ☐   7 × 8 = ☐   8 × 8 = ☐

8 × 8 = ☐   9 × 8 = ☐   2 × 8 = ☐   3 × 8 = ☐

4 × 8 = ☐   10 × 8 = ☐   8 × 8 = ☐   6 × 8 = ☐

9 × 8 = ☐   5 × 8 = ☐   4 × 8 = ☐   9 × 8 = ☐

6 × 8 = ☐   3 × 8 = ☐   6 × 8 = ☐   10 × 8 = ☐

2 × 8 = ☐   0 × 8 = ☐   1 × 8 = ☐   0 × 8 = ☐

10 × 8 = ☐   7 × 8 = ☐   9 × 8 = ☐   5 × 8 = ☐

7 × 8 = ☐   1 × 8 = ☐   5 × 8 = ☐   4 × 8 = ☐

1 × 8 = ☐   8 × 8 = ☐   0 × 8 = ☐   2 × 8 = ☐

Time ☐   Time ☐   Time ☐   Time ☐

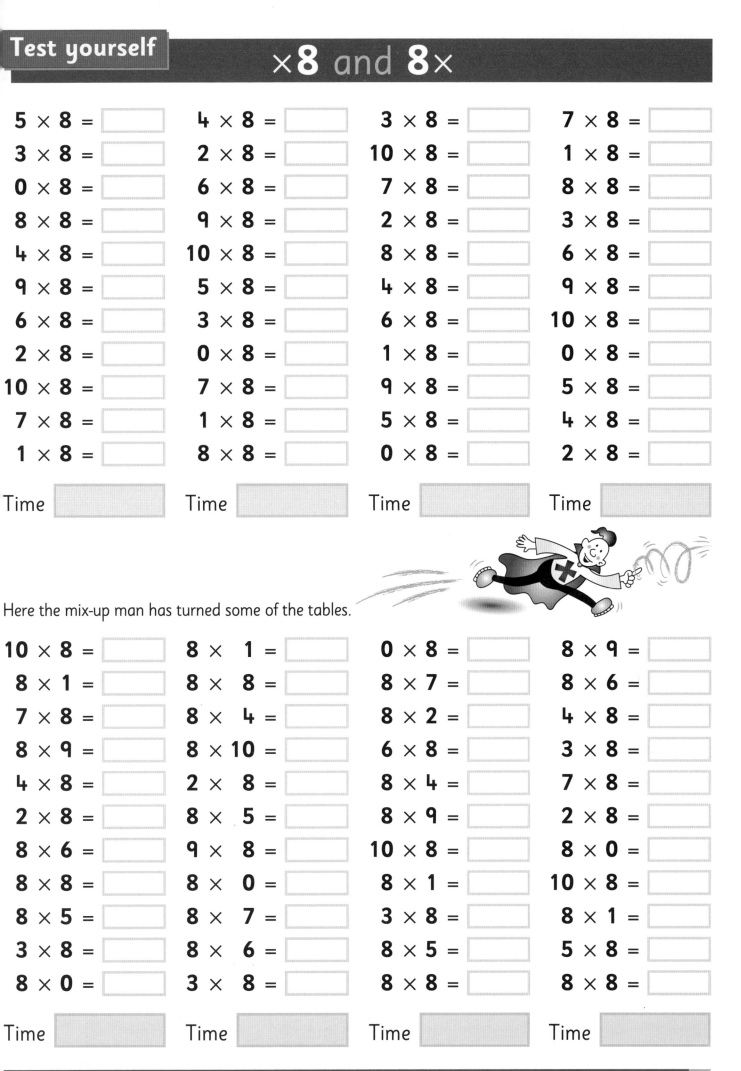

Here the mix-up man has turned some of the tables.

10 × 8 = ☐   8 × 1 = ☐   0 × 8 = ☐   8 × 9 = ☐

8 × 1 = ☐   8 × 8 = ☐   8 × 7 = ☐   8 × 6 = ☐

7 × 8 = ☐   8 × 4 = ☐   8 × 2 = ☐   4 × 8 = ☐

8 × 9 = ☐   8 × 10 = ☐   6 × 8 = ☐   3 × 8 = ☐

4 × 8 = ☐   2 × 8 = ☐   8 × 4 = ☐   7 × 8 = ☐

2 × 8 = ☐   8 × 5 = ☐   8 × 9 = ☐   2 × 8 = ☐

8 × 6 = ☐   9 × 8 = ☐   10 × 8 = ☐   8 × 0 = ☐

8 × 8 = ☐   8 × 0 = ☐   8 × 1 = ☐   10 × 8 = ☐

8 × 5 = ☐   8 × 7 = ☐   3 × 8 = ☐   8 × 1 = ☐

3 × 8 = ☐   8 × 6 = ☐   8 × 5 = ☐   5 × 8 = ☐

8 × 0 = ☐   3 × 8 = ☐   8 × 8 = ☐   8 × 8 = ☐

Time ☐   Time ☐   Time ☐   Time ☐

Mixed tests

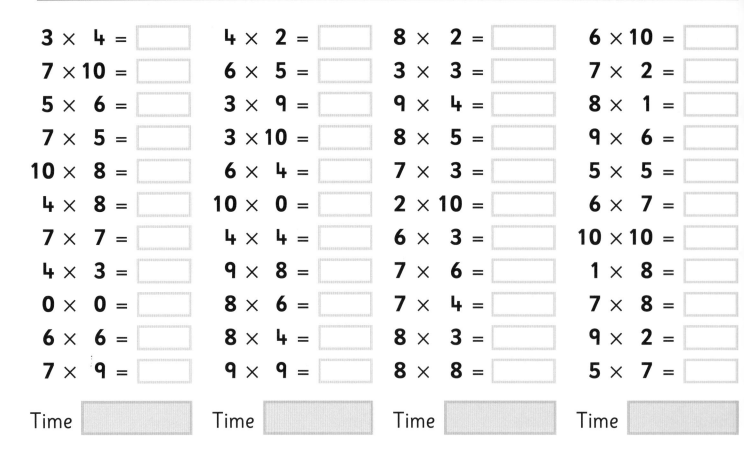

3 × 4 =

7 × 10 =

5 × 6 =

7 × 5 =

10 × 8 =

4 × 8 =

7 × 7 =

4 × 3 =

0 × 0 =

6 × 6 =

7 × 9 =

Time

4 × 2 =

6 × 5 =

3 × 9 =

3 × 10 =

6 × 4 =

10 × 0 =

4 × 4 =

9 × 8 =

8 × 6 =

8 × 4 =

9 × 9 =

Time

8 × 2 =

3 × 3 =

9 × 4 =

8 × 5 =

7 × 3 =

2 × 10 =

6 × 3 =

7 × 6 =

7 × 4 =

8 × 3 =

8 × 8 =

Time

6 × 10 =

7 × 2 =

8 × 1 =

9 × 6 =

5 × 5 =

6 × 7 =

10 × 10 =

1 × 8 =

7 × 8 =

9 × 2 =

5 × 7 =

Time

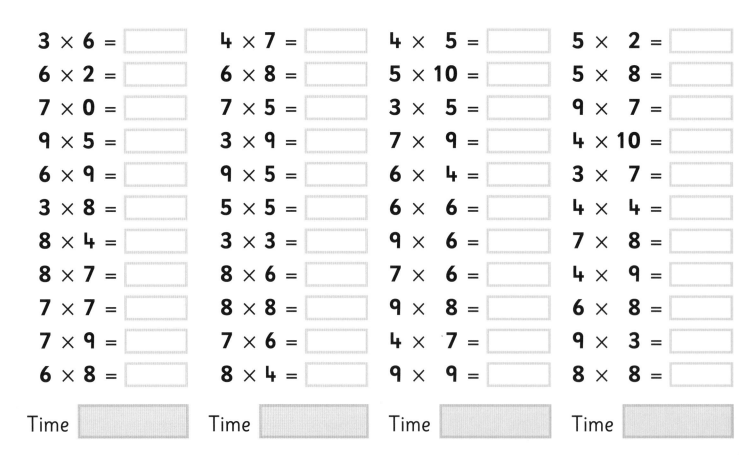

3 × 6 =

6 × 2 =

7 × 0 =

9 × 5 =

6 × 9 =

3 × 8 =

8 × 4 =

8 × 7 =

7 × 7 =

7 × 9 =

6 × 8 =

Time

4 × 7 =

6 × 8 =

7 × 5 =

3 × 9 =

9 × 5 =

5 × 5 =

3 × 3 =

8 × 6 =

8 × 8 =

7 × 6 =

8 × 4 =

Time

4 × 5 =

5 × 10 =

3 × 5 =

7 × 9 =

6 × 4 =

6 × 6 =

9 × 6 =

7 × 6 =

9 × 8 =

4 × 7 =

9 × 9 =

Time

5 × 2 =

5 × 8 =

9 × 7 =

4 × 10 =

3 × 7 =

4 × 4 =

7 × 8 =

4 × 9 =

6 × 8 =

9 × 3 =

8 × 8 =

Time

Mixed tests

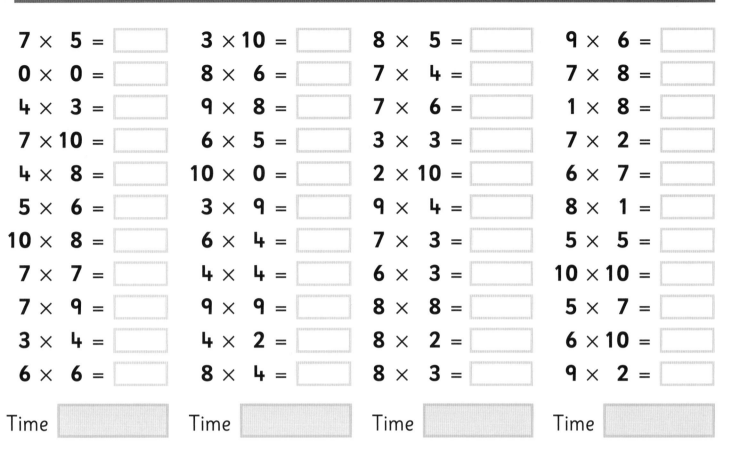

7 × 5 = ☐   3 × 10 = ☐   8 × 5 = ☐   9 × 6 = ☐
0 × 0 = ☐   8 × 6 = ☐   7 × 4 = ☐   7 × 8 = ☐
4 × 3 = ☐   9 × 8 = ☐   7 × 6 = ☐   1 × 8 = ☐
7 × 10 = ☐   6 × 5 = ☐   3 × 3 = ☐   7 × 2 = ☐
4 × 8 = ☐   10 × 0 = ☐   2 × 10 = ☐   6 × 7 = ☐
5 × 6 = ☐   3 × 9 = ☐   9 × 4 = ☐   8 × 1 = ☐
10 × 8 = ☐   6 × 4 = ☐   7 × 3 = ☐   5 × 5 = ☐
7 × 7 = ☐   4 × 4 = ☐   6 × 3 = ☐   10 × 10 = ☐
7 × 9 = ☐   9 × 9 = ☐   8 × 8 = ☐   5 × 7 = ☐
3 × 4 = ☐   4 × 2 = ☐   8 × 2 = ☐   6 × 10 = ☐
6 × 6 = ☐   8 × 4 = ☐   8 × 3 = ☐   9 × 2 = ☐

Time ☐   Time ☐   Time ☐   Time ☐

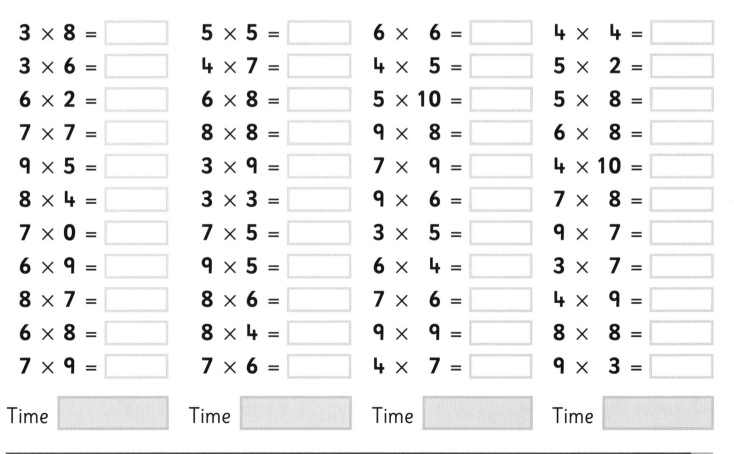

3 × 8 = ☐   5 × 5 = ☐   6 × 6 = ☐   4 × 4 = ☐
3 × 6 = ☐   4 × 7 = ☐   4 × 5 = ☐   5 × 2 = ☐
6 × 2 = ☐   6 × 8 = ☐   5 × 10 = ☐   5 × 8 = ☐
7 × 7 = ☐   8 × 8 = ☐   9 × 8 = ☐   6 × 8 = ☐
9 × 5 = ☐   3 × 9 = ☐   7 × 9 = ☐   4 × 10 = ☐
8 × 4 = ☐   3 × 3 = ☐   9 × 6 = ☐   7 × 8 = ☐
7 × 0 = ☐   7 × 5 = ☐   3 × 5 = ☐   9 × 7 = ☐
6 × 9 = ☐   9 × 5 = ☐   6 × 4 = ☐   3 × 7 = ☐
8 × 7 = ☐   8 × 6 = ☐   7 × 6 = ☐   4 × 9 = ☐
6 × 8 = ☐   8 × 4 = ☐   9 × 9 = ☐   8 × 8 = ☐
7 × 9 = ☐   7 × 6 = ☐   4 × 7 = ☐   9 × 3 = ☐

Time ☐   Time ☐   Time ☐   Time ☐

Summary

×3 table

0	× 3	=	0
1	× 3	=	3
2	× 3	=	6
3	× 3	=	9
4	× 3	=	12
5	× 3	=	15
6	× 3	=	18
7	× 3	=	21
8	× 3	=	24
9	× 3	=	27
10	× 3	=	30

×4 table

0	× 4	=	0
1	× 4	=	4
2	× 4	=	8
3	× 4	=	12
4	× 4	=	16
5	× 4	=	20
6	× 4	=	24
7	× 4	=	28
8	× 4	=	32
9	× 4	=	36
10	× 4	=	40

×9 table

0	× 9	=	0
1	× 9	=	9
2	× 9	=	18
3	× 9	=	27
4	× 9	=	36
5	× 9	=	45
6	× 9	=	54
7	× 9	=	63
8	× 9	=	72
9	× 9	=	81
10	× 9	=	90

×6 table

0	× 6	=	0
1	× 6	=	6
2	× 6	=	12
3	× 6	=	18
4	× 6	=	24
5	× 6	=	30
6	× 6	=	36
7	× 6	=	42
8	× 6	=	48
9	× 6	=	54
10	× 6	=	60

×7 table

0	× 7	=	0
1	× 7	=	7
2	× 7	=	14
3	× 7	=	21
4	× 7	=	28
5	× 7	=	35
6	× 7	=	42
7	× 7	=	49
8	× 7	=	56
9	× 7	=	63
10	× 7	=	70

×8 table

0	× 8	=	0
1	× 8	=	8
2	× 8	=	16
3	× 8	=	24
4	× 8	=	32
5	× 8	=	40
6	× 8	=	48
7	× 8	=	56
8	× 8	=	64
9	× 8	=	72
10	× 8	=	80

	Tick here		Tick here
I know my ×3 table.		I know my ×6 table.	
I know my ×4 table.		I know my ×7 table.	
I know my ×9 table.		I know my ×8 table.	

   Schofield & Sims Learn Your Times Tables 2